Step-by-Step Transformations
Turning Tomatoes into Ketchup

Dawn James

Cavendish Square

New York

Published in 2015 by Cavendish Square Publishing, LLC
243 5th Avenue, Suite 136, New York, NY 10016

Website: cavendishsq.com

This publication represents the opinions and views of the author based on his or her personal experience, knowledge, and research. The information in this book serves as a general guide only. The author and publisher have used their best efforts in preparing this book and disclaim liability rising directly or indirectly from the use and application of this book.

CPSIA Compliance Information: Batch #WS14CSQ

All websites were available and accurate when this book was sent to press.

Library of Congress Cataloging-in-Publication Data
James, Dawn.
Turning tomatoes into ketchup / Dawn James.
pages cm. — (Step-by-step transformations)
Includes bibliographical references and index.
ISBN 978-1-62713-010-3 (hardcover) ISBN 978-1-62713-011-0 (paperback) ISBN 978-1-62713-012-7 (ebook)
1. Ketchup—Juvenile literature. 2. Tomatoes—Juvenile literature. I. Title. II. Series: Step-by-step transformations.

TX819.K48J36 2014
664'.805642—dc23

2014002062

Editorial Director: Dean Miller
Editor: Amy Hayes
Copy Editor: Cynthia Roby
Art Director: Jeffrey Talbot
Designer: Joseph Macri
Photo Researcher: J8 Media
Production Manager: Jennifer Ryder-Talbot
Production Editor: David McNamara

The photographs in this book are used by permission and through the courtesy of: Cover photos by Copyright by Ata Mohammad Adnan/Flickr/Getty Images; AP Photo/Keith Srakocic; monticello/iStock/Thinkstock, 5; ©Mark Godfrey/The Image Works, 7; Tips Images/SuperStock, 9; FoodCollection/SuperStock, 11; Michael Rosenfeld/Maximilian S/Science Faction/SuperStock,13; Ableimages/SuperStock, 15; Ian O'Leary/Dorling Kindersley/Getty Images, 17; Norman Hollands/Photolibrary/Getty Images, 19; Ingo Wagner/picture-alliance/dpa/AP Images, 21; Back cover Schedivy Pictures Inc./The Image Bank/Getty Images.

Printed in the United States of America

Contents

Ketchup is made from tomatoes.

4

5

First, the tomatoes have to be **harvested**.

Big trucks are used to harvest many tomatoes at a time.

7

Next, the tomatoes are brought to a **factory**.

Workers inspect them to make sure they are good to eat.

9

Then, the tomatoes are heated and cooled in water.

This gets the tomatoes ready for peeling.

In the cool water, the skins come off easily.

After that, the tomatoes are placed in a **machine**.

The machine **removes** the seeds and hard parts of the tomatoes.

13

Now, the rest of the tomatoes
are a thick juice.

It is ready to be made
into ketchup.

The juice is put into a big pot.

Salt, vinegar, and other **ingredients** are added.

17

Then, the ingredients are mixed together.

As they mix, the pot heats up and cooks the **mixture**.

19

Finally, the ketchup is put into bottles.

It's ready to head to a store near you!

Words to Know

factory (FAK-tuh-ree) – a building that is filled with machines that make many things

harvest (HAR-vest) – to collect fruits or vegetables from the fields

ingredients (in-GREE-dee-entz) – parts that mix together to make a certain thing

machine (muh-SHEEN) – equipment with moving parts that are used to do a job

mixture (MIKS-cher) – something that has several ingredients

removes (ree-MOOVS) – takes away

Find Out More

Books

The Biography of Tomatoes

Adrianna Morganelli

Crabtree Publishing Company

From Tomato to Ketchup

Roberta Basel

Capstone

Website

Kids Growing Strong

Tomatoes, Tomatoes Everywhere!

www.kidsgrowingstrong.org/TomatoSeeds

Index